Rich Paul: A Trailblazing Sports Agent

Rich Paul, born on December 16, 1981, is indeed a prominent figure in the world of sports agency. He is best known for founding Klutch Sports Group, a sports management agency that represents some of the biggest names in the NBA and other professional sports leagues.

Rich Paul's journey to becoming a successful sports agent is a remarkable one. He grew up in a modest background in Cleveland, Ohio, and had a strong passion for basketball from a young age. He forged connections within the basketball world and started working as an agent. One of his early clients was his childhood friend and NBA superstar LeBron James.

Through his dedication, knowledge of the game, and strong personal relationships, Rich Paul built a reputation for himself and his agency. Klutch Sports Group has represented numerous NBA stars, including LeBron James, Anthony Davis, Ben Simmons, and others. Paul's ability to understand the needs and aspirations of his clients, coupled with his negotiation skills, has made him a force to be reckoned with in the sports industry.

Beyond his professional success, Rich Paul's life story serves as an inspiration to many. He has overcome obstacles and challenges to reach the pinnacle of his field, and his journey underscores the importance of hard work, resilience, and the power of genuine connections in achieving success.

Rich Paul's impact on the sports agency landscape cannot be overstated, and he continues to play a significant role in shaping the careers of some of the most talented athletes in the world of sports. His story is a testament to what can be achieved with determination, a strong vision, and a relentless pursuit of excellence.

Early Life

Rich Paul's journey began in the modest neighborhood of Glenville, located on the east side of Cleveland, Ohio. Raised in a one-bedroom apartment above his father's store, R & J Confectionery, he learned the value of hard work and perseverance from a young age. Tragically, his father's battle with cancer ended in 1999, leaving Paul to face life's challenges on his own.

Despite these obstacles, Paul's determination shone brightly. He attended Benedictine, a private Roman Catholic high school, thanks to his father's belief in the importance of education. After high school, he found mentorship from Andy Hyman, the owner of Distant Replays. It was during this time that he honed his skills in selling vintage jerseys, a business that started with him selling throwback jerseys out of his trunk in Cleveland. This entrepreneurial spirit would later play a pivotal role in his career.

In 2002, fate intervened when he crossed paths with NBA superstar LeBron James at the Akron–Canton Airport. Impressed by Paul's authenticity and passion for sports memorabilia, James purchased a Magic Johnson Lakers jersey and a Joe Namath Rams jersey from him. This chance meeting marked the beginning of a profound friendship and a future partnership in the world of sports.

Career

In the wake of the 2003 NBA draft, Rich Paul became an integral part of LeBron James' inner circle, joining childhood friends Maverick Carter and Randy Mims. This close-knit group embarked on a journey that would forever change the sports agency landscape. Paul's career trajectory took a significant leap when he started working under the guidance of Leon Rose, the agent who had negotiated LeBron James' contract extension with the Cleveland Cavaliers in 2006, at Creative Artists Agency (CAA).

In 2012, Rich Paul, in collaboration with LeBron James, made a momentous decision to break away from CAA and establish their own sports agency, Klutch Sports Group. The agency quickly gained prominence, and in 2013, Paul enlisted the experienced agent and attorney Mark Termini to lead NBA contract negotiations for Klutch. Under Termini's guidance, Klutch Sports thrived, representing a roster of 25 clients and brokering over $1 billion worth of NBA contracts.

Further expanding his influence in the sports industry, Rich Paul took on a role at United Talent Agency (UTA) in 2020. He was appointed to UTA's board of directors, solidifying his position as a force to be reckoned with in the sports world.

Championing Change

Rich Paul's advocacy against the NCAA's "Rich Paul Rule" is a significant example of his commitment to championing positive change within the sports industry. The rule, which would have required agents to hold a bachelor's degree, was widely seen as a way to limit the influence and success of agents like Paul, who had risen to prominence without a traditional college education.

Paul's vocal opposition to the rule drew attention to the potential inequities it would create. He argued that such a requirement could disproportionately affect individuals from underprivileged backgrounds, particularly people of color, who may face additional barriers in pursuing a college education. By taking a stand against this rule, he demonstrated a commitment to creating opportunities for those who might not have had access to the traditional paths within the sports industry.

Ultimately, Paul's advocacy efforts were successful in prompting the NCAA to reconsider and reverse the rule. This victory underscored the importance of diversity and inclusion within the sports agency profession and sent a powerful message that success in the industry should be determined by one's skills, knowledge, and abilities rather than arbitrary educational requirements.

Rich Paul's willingness to use his platform and influence to advocate for positive change reflects his dedication to leveling the playing field and ensuring that opportunities within the sports industry are accessible to a wider range of talented individuals, regardless of their educational background or socioeconomic status.

Rich Paul's commitment to making a positive impact on society extends beyond his work in sports agency, as demonstrated by his involvement in initiatives like "Klutch Conversations." This initiative, launched in collaboration with SocialWorks and General Mills in 2020, is a testament to his dedication to empowering young people through financial literacy.

Financial literacy is a crucial life skill that can have a profound impact on individuals' lives and their ability to make informed financial decisions. By partnering with organizations focused on education and social impact, Rich Paul and Klutch Sports Group took a proactive approach to address this important issue.

"Klutch Conversations" likely provided young people with valuable information and resources to better understand financial concepts, manage their finances, and plan for a more secure financial future. This kind of philanthropic effort can have a lasting positive influence on the lives of those who benefit from it, helping them build a foundation for financial well-being.

Rich Paul's involvement in initiatives like this not only reflects his desire to give back to the community but also highlights the potential for individuals in positions of influence to make a meaningful difference in the lives of others. By using his platform to promote financial literacy and empower young people, he contributes to creating a more financially educated and financially resilient generation, which can have wide-reaching positive effects on society as a whole.

Rich Paul's personal life, including his role as a devoted father to three children, demonstrates his commitment to both his family and his career. His ability to balance his professional success with his responsibilities as a parent underscores his dedication to all aspects of his life.

In 2021, Rich Paul's high-profile relationship with English singer-songwriter Adele became a topic of public interest, further increasing his visibility in the public eye. Such relationships can often bring added scrutiny and attention, but Rich Paul has continued to maintain his focus on his career and advocacy efforts.

Rich Paul's recognition on prestigious lists like the "Ebony Power 100 List" and Forbes' "World's Most Powerful Sports Agents" list highlights the impact he has made in the sports agency world. His story is indeed an inspiring one, emphasizing the importance of determination, resilience, and the pursuit of one's dreams.

As he continues to shape the future of sports agency and advocate for positive change, Rich Paul's journey serves as an example of what can be achieved through hard work, vision, and a commitment to making a difference in the world of sports and beyond.

A Trailblazing Sports Agent

Indeed, Rich Paul's journey in the world of sports agency is a testament to his ambition and dedication. As the founder of Klutch Sports Group, he has blazed a trail that has reshaped the sports agency industry and set a new standard for what can be achieved. His ability to build authentic relationships with athletes and advocate for their interests has made him a trusted figure in the world of professional sports.

Rich Paul's impact goes beyond just representing athletes; he has also been a force for positive change, advocating for fairness and inclusivity within the industry. His successful efforts to challenge and reverse the NCAA's "Rich Paul Rule" is a prime example of his commitment to creating opportunities for all, regardless of background or education.

His story serves as an inspiration not only to aspiring sports agents but also to anyone with a dream and the determination to pursue it. Rich Paul's remarkable journey reminds us that with passion, hard work, and a focus on building meaningful relationships, one can achieve great success and leave a lasting impact on their industry.

Rich Paul's advocacy for change within the sports industry, particularly in his successful challenge against the NCAA's "Rich Paul Rule," is a powerful example of his commitment to breaking down barriers and promoting equity. The "Rich Paul Rule," which initially required agents to hold a bachelor's degree, was seen as an attempt to restrict access to the industry and limit the success of individuals like Paul, who had taken unconventional paths to their careers.

Paul's outspoken opposition to the rule highlighted its potential to disproportionately impact underprivileged individuals, especially people of color, who may face additional obstacles in pursuing higher education. His advocacy efforts played a pivotal role in the NCAA's decision to reconsider and ultimately reverse the regulation.

By challenging the "Rich Paul Rule," Rich Paul underscored the importance of inclusivity and equal opportunity within the sports industry. His actions sent a clear message that success in the field should be determined by merit, skill, and dedication rather than arbitrary educational requirements. This stance not only benefited him but also opened doors for others who may have faced similar barriers.

Rich Paul's dedication to championing change and his willingness to use his platform to advocate for fairness and equal opportunity have had a positive impact on the sports industry, contributing to a more inclusive and equitable environment for athletes, agents, and aspiring professionals alike.

Rich Paul's commitment to making a positive impact on society is exemplified by initiatives like "Klutch Conversations." This program, launched in collaboration with SocialWorks and General Mills in 2020, showcases his dedication to empowering young people through financial literacy.

Financial literacy is a critical life skill that can empower individuals to make informed financial decisions and secure their financial future. By partnering with organizations focused on education and social impact, Rich Paul and Klutch Sports Group have taken a proactive approach to address this important issue.

"Klutch Conversations" likely provided young people with valuable knowledge and resources to better understand financial concepts, manage their finances, and plan for a more secure financial future. Such initiatives have the potential to make a significant and lasting positive impact on the lives of those who participate, helping them build a strong foundation for financial well-being.

Rich Paul's involvement in projects like this demonstrates his commitment to giving back to the community and using his platform to uplift and inspire the next generation. By promoting financial literacy and empowerment, he contributes to creating a more financially educated and financially resilient generation, which can have far-reaching positive effects on society as a whole.

Personal Life and Influence

Rich Paul's personal life and relationships, including his high-profile connection with Adele, have indeed garnered significant attention from the public. His ability to connect with individuals from diverse backgrounds and walks of life highlights his broad appeal and interpersonal skills.

Being included in the 2020 "Ebony Power 100 List" and ranking fourth on Forbes' "World's Most Powerful Sports Agents" list in 2022 are clear indications of the enduring impact Rich Paul has had on both the sports and entertainment industries. These recognitions underscore his influence and success, not just as a sports agent but as a figure who has made a significant mark on various facets of the professional world.

Rich Paul's story serves as an example of how passion, determination, and the ability to build authentic relationships can lead to remarkable success and influence. His achievements and continued impact in various domains, along with his ability to connect with people from all walks of life, showcase the multifaceted nature of his influence and the wide-reaching significance of his work.

Legacy and Future

As Rich Paul continues to shape the future of sports agency, his legacy stands as a testament to the limitless potential of determination and vision. His unwavering commitment to creating opportunities and driving positive change will undoubtedly inspire generations to come.

Rich Paul's journey from a one-bedroom apartment in Cleveland to the pinnacle of the sports world serves as a reminder that, with passion, perseverance, and the right connections, one can overcome adversity and achieve greatness. His story is a testament to the power of believing in oneself, forging meaningful relationships, and reshaping industries for the better.

In conclusion, Rich Paul's life and career are a remarkable narrative of resilience, success, and advocacy for change. His impact transcends the sports industry, offering a blueprint for aspiring agents and a source of inspiration for those seeking to make a difference in the world. Rich Paul's legacy is still unfolding, and his influence will continue to shape the future of sports and beyond.

Building Bridges and Shaping the Future

Rich Paul's journey is indeed a testament to the transformative power of determination, resilience, and the significance of authentic connections. His success in the sports agency industry has not only made him a prominent figure but has also elevated the role of a sports agent to unprecedented heights. His commitment to his clients and his relentless pursuit of excellence have set a standard for others in the industry to aspire to.

By breaking down barriers, advocating for change, and using his platform to make a positive impact on society, Rich Paul has not only achieved personal success but has also contributed to shaping the future of the sports agency world and beyond. His story serves as an inspiration to aspiring professionals, demonstrating that with hard work, dedication, and the ability to forge meaningful relationships, one can overcome obstacles and achieve remarkable success.

Rich Paul's influence extends beyond the sports industry, highlighting the broader impact that individuals can have when they use their success and platform to champion change and make a positive difference in the world. His journey reminds us that success is not just about personal achievement but also about the opportunities one creates for others and the legacy one leaves behind.

Empowering Athletes

Rich Paul's dedication to empowering the athletes he represents goes beyond the typical agent-client relationship. He has demonstrated a deep commitment to the well-being and success of his clients by serving as a mentor, confidant, and advocate for their interests. This unique approach has not only resulted in lucrative contracts but has also fostered personal growth and development among his clients.

By providing guidance, support, and a genuine understanding of their needs and aspirations, Rich Paul has helped his clients navigate the often complex world of professional sports. His willingness to stand up for their rights and advocate for their interests has earned him their trust and loyalty.

Empowering athletes in this way not only benefits the individuals he represents but also contributes to the overall improvement of the sports industry. It highlights the importance of a holistic approach to athlete representation, one that goes beyond financial negotiations to address the personal and professional development of athletes.

Rich Paul's commitment to empowering athletes is a significant part of his legacy, showcasing the positive impact that a sports agent can have on the lives and careers of the athletes they represent. His approach serves as a model for others in the industry, emphasizing the importance of building meaningful and supportive relationships with clients to help them reach their full potential both on and off the field.

Rich Paul's influence in the sports industry extends well beyond contract negotiations. He has been a pioneer in implementing innovative marketing strategies and branding initiatives for the athletes he represents. His ability to help athletes build lasting legacies off the court or field has reshaped how sports professionals engage with their fans and the broader public.

One of Rich Paul's notable innovations has been harnessing the power of social media and leveraging his extensive network to elevate his clients' profiles. In today's digital age, social media has become a crucial tool for athletes to connect with their fans, build their personal brands, and make a broader impact beyond their respective sports. Rich Paul's understanding of this dynamic has allowed his clients to effectively utilize social media platforms, reach a wider audience, and engage with their followers authentically.

By guiding athletes in these branding and marketing efforts, Rich Paul has helped them create meaningful and lasting connections with their fans and the public. This not only benefits the athletes in terms of their marketability but also allows them to make a positive impact in areas beyond sports, such as philanthropy and advocacy.

Rich Paul's innovative approach to athlete representation underscores the evolving nature of the sports industry and highlights the importance of adapting to new technologies and platforms. His influence in this regard has not only benefited his clients but has also set a precedent for how athletes can leverage their personal brands to create a broader and more lasting impact in the world.

Rich Paul's partnership with Adele, a globally recognized English singer-songwriter, is indeed a testament to his ability to transcend boundaries and connect with individuals from diverse backgrounds. It showcases his magnetic personality and his skill in bridging gaps between different worlds, such as the sports and entertainment industries.

Their union represents the convergence of two distinct but influential spheres—sports and music. It not only captivates the public's attention but also symbolizes the power of genuine connections and shared interests. Rich Paul's ability to build such connections not only benefits him personally but also opens doors for collaboration and cross-industry opportunities that can have a broad-reaching impact.

As a global icon, Rich Paul's influence extends beyond traditional boundaries and industries, highlighting the potential for individuals with diverse backgrounds and interests to create meaningful connections and make a positive impact on a worldwide scale. His ability to navigate different worlds and bring people together underscores the importance of authenticity and relationship-building in achieving success and influence on a global stage.

Rich Paul's inclusion in the "Ebony Power 100 List" in 2020 and his notable ranking on Forbes' "World's Most Powerful Sports Agents" list in 2022 are indeed significant honors and recognitions. These accolades underscore his exceptional impact on the sports and entertainment industries and serve as validations of his trailblazing and trendsetting work.

Being featured in the "Ebony Power 100 List" recognizes his influence and contributions not only to the world of sports agency but also to broader societal and cultural conversations. This list typically highlights individuals who have made substantial contributions to African American culture and society.

His ranking on Forbes' list of powerful sports agents reinforces his standing as a prominent figure within his industry. It reflects his ability to navigate the complex world of athlete representation, negotiate high-value contracts, and advocate for the rights and interests of his clients.

These honors and recognitions are a testament to Rich Paul's outstanding achievements and his enduring impact on the sports and entertainment landscapes. They solidify his position as a leader and innovator in his field and underscore the significance of his contributions to the industry and society as a whole.

Rich Paul's ongoing legacy is indeed an enduring source of inspiration for many. His journey from humble beginnings to a position of unparalleled influence in the sports agency landscape exemplifies the essence of the American Dream. It serves as a powerful reminder that, with resilience, vision, and unwavering commitment, individuals can overcome barriers and redefine what success means to them.

His story is a testament to the power of authentic relationships, the value of mentorship, and the limitless potential of determination. Rich Paul's legacy extends far beyond his personal achievements; it is a beacon of hope and motivation for those who aspire to make a difference and leave a lasting impact on the world.

As he continues to shape the sports industry and advocate for positive change, Rich Paul's legacy will undoubtedly inspire future generations of athletes, agents, and individuals from all walks of life. His story demonstrates that with dedication and a strong sense of purpose, individuals can overcome adversity, break down barriers, and achieve their goals, no matter how ambitious they may be. Rich Paul's ongoing journey is a testament to the idea that the pursuit of excellence knows no bounds, and his legacy will continue to resonate with those who seek to follow in his footsteps.

Printed in Great Britain
by Amazon

29268214R00020